THE SECRET OF THE RAVEN

THE
SECRET
OF
THE
RAVEN

Mike Bell

Beacon Hill Press of Kansas City
Kansas City, Missouri

Copyright 1997
by Beacon Hill Press of Kansas City

ISBN 083-411-6472

Printed in the United States of America

Editor: Bruce Nuffer
Assistant Editor: Micah Moseley
Cover Design: Mike Walsh

Illustrations: Dave Howard

Note: This book is part of the *Understanding Christian Mission,* Children's Mission Education curriculum. It is designed for use in Year 2, The Bible in Mission. This study year examines the importance of the Bible in the mission enterprise. This book was chosen for use in this year because it gives children insights into the importance of the Bible to missionaries as well as the unsaved. This book was based on several true stories. Avee's healing is based on a missionary's experience in Haiti, as well as an account in India in 1994. The angelic warrior episode is based on the true experience of Brad and Joelyn Grant, former missionaries near the southern jungle area of Colombia.

10   9   8   7   6   5   4   3   2   1

Contents

THE
SECRET
OF
THE
RAVEN

1

Hunted

The young hunter aimed his bow carefully. He pulled back the string and let the poison-tipped arrow fly. The feathers of a bird ruffled as the arrow sailed less than an inch above its head.

"Missed again," Avee (ah-VEE) said angrily.

His friend, Dav (DAHV), chuckled, "At least you ruffled its feathers this time."

"It's not funny," Avee said. "A chief must be a great hunter."

"You're not chief yet, Avee. Your father is still young. There is time for you to become a hunter before you follow him as village chief."

The two young boys had risen early for their hunt deep in the Brazilian jungle.

"It's getting late. We should be heading back," Dav said. He turned to walk back toward their village. A sound caused him to pause and listen. Avee listened too.

It came again, the crunch of leaves under something's foot. Using hand signals, Avee pointed in the direction of the sound. He remembered an important lesson his father had taught him about hunting in the jungle.

"Avee, when you are hunting," his father had said, "be careful not to become the hunted. The animals you hunt make noise as they flee. But listen for the sound of something moving toward you. Listen for twigs or branches breaking under foot. If you hear it twice, be ready. If you hear it a third time, run. You have become the hunted."

Avee and Dav stood silently, their hearts racing as they strained to hear. The jungle also grew quiet as if waiting and listening.

Snap! The sound came a third time.

"Run," Avee screamed, pushing Dav in front of him.

Stumbling through the brush, they found the trail they had been following.

"Faster, Dav! It's after us!" Avee yelled, panting.

Neither boy dared look back. They continued running until they thought their lungs would burst.

The trail turned sharply left along the top of a shallow ravine. Neither boy saw the dark shape leap from the ravine onto the trail behind them.

The shape grabbed Avee from behind so swiftly Dav heard nothing. Dav kept running as fast as his tired legs would go. When he was a hundred yards from the village, he looked behind him. Avee was gone.

"Avee!" Dav called breathlessly. He walked slowly back down the path. But after a few steps, a movement in the brush ahead caught his eye.

"Avee? Avee, is that you?"

No answer. Just the sound of a twig snapping.

Dav didn't wait to hear the sound a second or third time but turned and ran for the village, yelling for help.

The shape moved out of its hiding place in the brush, following the path back to the shallow ravine. If anyone had been watching, they would have seen that the shape was not a wild animal but a man.

At the edge, the man looked down at Avee, lying on the bottom of the ravine. A smile crossed the man's lips.

"Ahhhhhh." A low moan came from Avee as he tried to move.

The smile vanished from the man's face. Suddenly the voices of villagers echoed in the jungle, calling Avee's name.

"Another time, young chief-to-be," the man said under his breath. He then disappeared into the darkness of the jungle.

2

Can't Sleep

Seventy-five miles from Avee's village, the Hunters settled into their rooms at the Riverside Hotel in Manaus (mah-NOWS), Brazil. Manaus sits at the intersection of Brazil's largest rivers, the Negro and the Amazon. It is the gateway to the Amazon jungle of northern Brazil.

Lee Hunter and his wife, Rusti, with their kids and a nephew, had come from Oklahoma City in the United States. They traveled with 10 others from their church in Oklahoma. The group had come on a Work and Witness trip to help set up a clinic in Manaus. As a medical doctor and nurse, Dr. Hunter and his wife were to help get the clinic ready for use.

"Liz, close the window shutters and get into bed," Josh, her older brother, said.

Liz Hunter, 9 years old, was almost as tall as her 11½-year-old brother. Though she secretly liked the way Josh always tried to look after her, she never let him know it.

"Oh, Josh, how can you talk about sleep? Our hotel is just a few miles from the Amazon jungle. Isn't it exciting?"

"Actually, 'rain forest' is a more accurate description of the surrounding countryside," Randal, Liz and Josh's 12-year-old cousin, said.

"Thank you, professor," said Liz with a mock accent. She closed the shutters and plopped down onto her bed.

Both of Randal's parents were university professors. They were spending the summer in the Middle East doing research. Since some of their studies would take them into dangerous areas, they felt it best that Randal spend the summer with his cousins. The idea did not thrill Josh and Liz.

Randal was usually a pain. He liked everything done his way, and he was always right. He didn't just *think* he was right; he *was* always right. Randal was a walking encyclopedia.

"Elizabeth," Randal liked to use everyone's proper full name, "if you and Joshua will pay attention on this trip, I will teach you many things."

"Oh brother," Josh said, putting a pillow over his head. "Can we wait until tomorrow for our first lesson?" He was in the top bunk above Randal. Liz's bed was across the small room under the window.

Liz reached up and pulled the cord on the single lightbulb hanging from the ceiling. The room went black.

"I'm simply saying," Randal went on, "that you both should take full advantage of this wonderful opportunity. This 'Work and . . . ' What do you call this trip?"

"Work and Witness," Liz answered.

"Ah yes, 'Work and Witness.' Well, I see this trip as a good chance to advance my learning. But I guess your parents have some religious reason for our being

13

here," Randal said.

"The 'religious reason,' as you call it, Randal, is the whole purpose of the trip," Liz explained. "Weren't you listening to the Bible verses Dad read just before bed? We're here to let others see the love that Jesus has for them through the work we do."

Randal started to answer, but Josh cut him off. "Shhhh," he whispered. "I heard something outside the window."

"Oh, Josh, you're just trying to . . ." Liz stopped short. She heard the noise too.

The sound, like a squeaky hinge opening, caused all three to stare wide-eyed at the window. Liz, whose bed was just below, ran to Josh's bunk. Looking, they saw the shutters on the window slowly open, but it was too dark to see anyone.

"Should we yell for Dad?" Liz whispered.

"N . . . n . . . n . . . no," Josh stammered. "It's ju . . . ju . . . just the wi . . . wi . . . wind."

"I . . . I . . . I . . . I quite agree, Joshua. Ye . . . ye . . . yelling would be a chi . . . chi . . . childish thing to do," Randal said from behind his pillow.

Suddenly, something fell from the windowsill and landed in the middle of the room.

"YEEEEE!! YEEEEE!! YEEEEE!!" shrieked the thing.

Whatever it was, it was alive!

Childish or not, all three kids did the same thing. "AHHHHHHHHHHHHHHHHH!"

3

Call for Help

Doors flew open, and the children heard the sound of running feet on the wooden floors of the hallway. Dr. Hunter burst through the door of the children's room, with Mrs. Hunter right behind.

"Children, what's wrong?" Mrs. Hunter said, reaching to pull the cord on the lightbulb. Eyes squinted at the sudden burst of light.

Liz let out a gasp. There in the middle of the room was a large monkey. It stood with its hands on its hips, staring curiously at everyone.

The hotel manager squeezed through the crowd of people gathered in the doorway. "Oh, Santo, you bad, bad monkey," he said, pointing his finger at the furry animal.

Santo turned to look at the manager and made a rather rude sound with his lips and tongue. He then jumped onto Liz's bed and out the window.

"I'm so sorry," the manager said, wiping his sweaty face. "Santo is my daughter's pet. Sneaking into rooms and scaring our guests is his favorite game. I think I will feed him to the crocodiles. Please accept my apology. It will not happen again."

Mrs. Hunter burst out laughing. Soon everyone in the room, including the children, were doing the same.

But soon, shouting interrupted the laughter. From down the hall someone was calling, "Dr. Hunter! Dr. Hunter! Come quickly! There is someone calling for you over the radio."

"Do you think it's Paul?" Mrs. Hunter asked, looking at her husband.

"Yes, but why would he be calling so late?"

A man led Dr. Hunter to a small office. A dusty radio sat on the corner of an old metal desk.

Paul Wilks, a full-time missionary in the Amazon jungle, was Dr. Hunter's best friend. They had grown up together in Oklahoma. They had even spent a year working on the mission field before Dr. Hunter went to medical school. Paul was one of the reasons the Work and Witness team had come to Manaus.

"Paul, is that you?" asked Dr. Hunter into the microphone. "This is Lee. Can you read me? Over."

The radio crackled.

"I read you loud and clear, Lee. It's great to hear your voice."

"It's good hearing yours too. But why are you calling so late? Is there a problem?"

"I'm afraid so. There's been an accident here in the village. The chief's son is badly hurt. He can't move at all. I'm afraid if we try to carry him out of the jungle for help, we will do even more damage."

"You're right, Paul. You shouldn't move him until a doctor examines him. Is there any way for me to get to you?"

"That's why I called. My mission station is just a six-hour boat ride to the north. The village is five miles into the jungle from there."

"Great! I'll hire a boat first thing in the morning. I'll see you by tomorrow afternoon."

Mrs. Hunter had followed her husband into the office and was listening to the conversation. "You'll need a nurse along, won't you?" she asked.

"Say, Paul, I'd like to bring Rusti along to help," Dr. Hunter said into the microphone.

"And the children," his wife added.

Dr. Hunter thought for a moment, then began again. "Paul, what do you think about bringing the kids too?"

"They'll be leaving the comforts of the city, but it's a safe trip," Paul answered. "It would be good for everyone to see what goes on in a jungle mission."

"Great! You can look for all of us sometime tomorrow afternoon. By the way, what is the boy's name? We'd like to have everyone here begin praying for him."

"His name is Avee," Paul said. "He is the chief's only son."

4

Floating Danger

Dr. Hunter rose early the next morning. The hotel manager helped him hire a boat to take the Hunters to the mission station. The doctor arrived back at the hotel in time to gather the team members for morning devotions.

Burt Lewis, a carpenter and the leader of the work team, stood to begin the devotion time.

"As I was reading my Bible this morning, two verses stood out. I wanted to share them with all of you. They're from the Gospel of John, chapter 14, verses 12 and 13.

"I tell you the truth, anyone who has faith in me will do what I have been doing. He will do even greater things than these, because I am going to the Father. And I will do whatever you ask in my name, so that the Son may bring glory to the Father."

Burt cleared his throat and continued. "Jesus is not saying that we get whatever we pray for just by saying, 'In Jesus' name.' But He does say He wants to work through us to bring glory and honor to God the Father. If we will ask Him, He will show us what He wants us to do, and He will give us the power to do it. Through these verses, I feel the Lord saying that this Work and Witness trip has a special purpose to bring glory to God."

"Amen," several of the team members said. Others nodded their heads in agreement.

Burt finished by saying, "Let's pray for our work here in town. And let's remember the Hunters' trip into the jungle."

One by one they began to pray. Everyone held hands. Randal got up to leave, but two of the team members grabbed his hands before he could get away.

Mrs. Hunter prayed last. "Father God, we ask that You help everything to work out for Your glory and honor on our trip today. Give us faith to trust You always. Help us to be Your light where there is darkness. In Jesus' name we have prayed. Amen."

"Amen," the rest of the group said.

It was a short walk from the hotel down to the boat docks on the Negro River. The Hunters and Randal each had a backpack and sleeping bag. Dr. Hunter also carried a large duffel bag filled with medical supplies.

"This is our boat?" Liz asked, standing with the others waiting to get on board. She sounded disappointed.

"What were you expecting, a cruise ship?" Josh asked.

The old 40-foot riverboat sat low in the water. It smelled of dead fish and gasoline. The paint had chipped off long ago. Even so, you could still make out the name on the front, *Bo Bo.*

"*Bo Bo?* Who would name a boat *Bo Bo?*" Liz asked.

"Be quiet, Liz," Josh scolded. "The captain probably named it after his wife or something."

Just then the boat's captain poked his head out of the cabin. He gave a big, toothless grin as he waved for the Hunters to come aboard.

"So, who recommended this mighty sailing ship, dear?" Mrs. Hunter asked her husband.

"The manager of our hotel."

"Is that the same hotel manager who owns the attacking monkey?" she teased.

"Let's just get on board, shall we?" Dr. Hunter said.

Mrs. Hunter giggled as she directed the children down the steps and onto the boat. They pushed away from the dock and headed north up the Negro River.

"I think we should ask for the Lord's protection as we're traveling," Dr. Hunter said, taking his wife's hand.

Randal made a face. "We already prayed back at the hotel; why waste our time doing it again?"

"Randal, prayer is never a waste of time," Mrs. Hunter said. "The Bible says to do it all the time. Besides, I think this boat could use some extra prayer."

"Ah, yes, the Bible. Why do you all quote so much from a book written thousands of years ago? What could it possibly have to say to us today?" Randal asked.

"You're right, the Bible is very old," Dr. Hunter said, "but it still reveals God's direction for our lives today."

"It also points the way to knowing Jesus," Josh added.

Randal wasn't convinced, but he bowed his head anyway. Dr. Hunter prayed for the boat and their trip up the river.

Josh, Liz, and Randal sat on the roof of the boat's cabin, watching the river. But by noon the sun was so hot that they sought shelter in the cabin.

"I think it's hotter in here," Liz said. "At least on the roof there was a breeze."

The boat captain, who could speak a little English, said, "You take swim. No more be hot."

Josh looked at Mrs. Hunter. "Could we, Mom?"

"Is it safe?" she asked the captain.

The captain just smiled his toothless grin and said, "Take swim, no be hot."

She looked at Dr. Hunter, who shrugged. "I suppose it would be OK. But won't that slow us down?" he said to the captain.

"Must stop and cool engine. Ten minutes."

The captain shut the engine down to a slow crawl. Josh and Liz changed into their swimsuits. Randal refused to swim in the dark green water. A few minutes later Josh and Liz screamed wildly as they jumped off the back of the boat into the cool river.

No one saw the two green shapes gliding along the river toward the boat.

5

Crocodile Cowboy

Liz had enough. She pulled herself out of the water, using a rope tied to the boat.

As she dried off, Josh called to her. "Come on, Liz, get back in. I promise not to dunk you again."

Liz pretended not to hear as she bent over to dry her hair. Then something in the river caught her eye. Squinting against the sun, she saw two long shapes moving in the water just a few feet from the boat.

Suddenly, she realized what she saw. Josh still swam behind the boat. She did the first thing that came to mind—"AHHHHHHHHHHHHHHHHH!"

"Josh! Crocodiles! Get out of the water!" Liz screamed.

But to Liz's amazement, Josh reached out and grabbed one of the reptiles around the neck. The captain, who had run out of the cabin with his gun, stood next to her, laughing.

"Loggers cut down trees. Some float down river. Not crocodile—logs," the captain said.

Josh held on to the boat's rope and rode on top of one of the logs. "Hey, Liz, look at me. I'm a crocodile cowboy."

Dr. Hunter chuckled, "Well, jungle man, I think that's enough crocodile wrestling for one day." He reached out to help his son out of the water.

"We will no doubt encounter a crocodile before our trip is over. But I think it's unlikely before we move deeper into the rain forest," Randal said, peering over the top of the book he was reading.

"Big crocks, long way off. No big crocks here," the captain said as he started the engine. "Maybe we see little crocks, though."

"How big is a little crock?" Mrs. Hunter asked.

The captain paced off 6 feet, then smiled his toothless grin. "That a little crock."

Mrs. Hunter turned pale. "There will be no more swimming in the river." No one argued.

The *Bo Bo* continued up the Negro River. Dark, oily smoke puffed from its engine. When the captain turned east, up a smaller river flowing from the Negro, he held up a finger.

"Be at mission, one hour."

Josh, Liz, and Randal crowded to the front of the boat. They wanted to be the first to see the camp. Dr. and Mrs. Hunter rechecked the medical supply bag, then joined the children at the front.

Exactly one hour later, Josh pointed and shouted, "There's the mission."

A long, wooden dock stretched 20 feet out into the river. A man stood alone on the dock, waving his arms.

"Dad, is that Uncle Paul?" Liz asked excitedly. She and Josh had grown up calling their father's best friend Uncle.

"It sure is."

Paul Wilks leaped onto the deck and embraced Dr. Hunter before the boat even stopped moving.

"You made good time. You never know what will happen with this old pirate," he said. He patted the captain's back affectionately.

Paul Wilks was taller than Dr. Hunter. Months of hiking in the jungle made him physically fit. He wore a sweat-stained T-shirt and shorts. His sandy-colored hair stuck out from under a baseball cap.

"It will be dark soon. Let's store your gear in the sleeping hut. Then we'll eat."

"Good, I'm starving," Josh said.

"I don't see any of the tribe around. Are you alone here, Paul?" Mrs. Hunter asked.

"Just for this evening. They've all gone to the village to keep watch over the chief's son."

"Has there been any change in his condition?" Dr. Hunter asked.

"He still can't move. We'll go to him in the morning. The village is only five miles north, but through the jungle it will take a couple of hours."

The mission station consisted of two huts and a large tent. Paul led them to one of the huts.

"Hey, the walls of this hut are cloth," Josh said.

"Actually it's mosquito netting," Paul explained. He pulled back a fold and gestured for everyone to go inside. "The hut has no walls, so the breeze can blow through. The netting allows you to sleep without being eaten alive by insects."

Paul pointed to the hammocks stretching between the poles supporting the roof. "You'll sleep in these. They take some getting used to, but they're comfortable. The mosquito netting helps with flying critters, but it doesn't always keep out the creepy crawlies."

"Creepy crawlies?" Liz asked.

"I imagine he is referring to reptiles or rodents of the Amazon rain forest, including—"

Liz interrupted Randal. "Never mind, I don't want to know."

"Leave your bags here. We'll get the fires going and see what feast we can put together for dinner," Paul said.

Everyone followed him out of the hut except Mrs. Hunter. She removed a pair of tweezers from the medical supply bag. A splinter from the boat had lodged itself into her palm. She caught up with the group after it was extracted.

As she left, an Indian tribesman moved silently from behind a tree and up to the hut. He had been secretly watching the camp, waiting for the Hunters to leave. He lifted the netting, stepped inside, and began looking through the Hunters' bags. He quickly found what he came for. He lifted the item onto his back, stepped out of the hut, and disappeared into the jungle.

6

Which Way to Go?

"That's impossible! It can't be gone," Dr. Hunter said in amazement. He ran back to the hut with his wife.

He pulled back the netting and walked in. He pointed his flashlight around. "I set it right here just an hour ago."

"I know. I opened it just before we walked out," Mrs. Hunter said. "When I came back a few minutes ago, I saw someone had moved our bags, and it was gone."

"What's gone?" Josh asked breathlessly. He had run to catch up with his parents. Liz, Randal, and Paul were just behind him.

"The medical supply bag," Dr. Hunter answered.

"You mean it just vanished?" Liz asked.

"Obviously it didn't vanish, Elizabeth," Randal said, squeezing past Josh and Liz to get a closer look. "Someone has taken it. I suggest we not touch anything until we have thoroughly searched for clues."

"Paul, do you have any ideas about this?" Dr. Hunter asked.

Everyone turned to look at Paul, who was staring into the darkness of the jungle.

"Kren," he said.

"Kren? What's a Kren?" Josh asked.

"Not a what, a who," Paul answered, turning back to the others. "He's the tribe's shaman."

"Shaman? You mean like a witch doctor?" Mrs. Hunter asked.

"That's right. The Atroari (ah-TROO-ah-ree) believe that the shaman can keep evil spirits away. He and the chief are the most important elders in the village."

"So why would this Kren want to take our medical supplies?" Dr. Hunter asked.

"During my first meetings with the tribe, Kren ignored me. Usually the Indians are very curious about outsiders. But Kren acted as if he didn't notice me, as if he had been around outsiders before. But when the chief and his son took a liking to me, I could tell Kren wasn't happy."

"Did he threaten you?" Dr. Hunter asked.

"Not directly. My work here is to share the love of Christ with the people. I am learning more of their language so I can share the gospel with them. Other missionaries are working to write their language. When they finish, we will translate the Bible and teach the Atroari to read it. The Holy Spirit has blessed our work. In a few months, I will be able to tell the chief more about Jesus."

"How has he responded to what you have told him so far?" Dr. Hunter asked.

"He's shown a lot of interest. Often a missionary must spend years with a tribe before anyone shows interest in the gospel. But it's as if the Lord had been preparing the chief's heart even before I arrived. The chief has even encouraged others in the village to listen. That's when Kren got mad. He began saying the spirits would be angry because I had come to the village."

"So when the chief's son got hurt," Josh said, "Kren must have told everyone it was an angry spirit."

"That's exactly what he did, Josh," Paul said. "But by the grace of God the chief still believes I'm a friend. He agreed to let me call you for help."

"So you think Kren is trying to make you look bad. He took the medical supplies so we could not help the chief's son," Dr. Hunter said.

"I think it's deeper than that. I believe Kren wants to prove to the village that his spirits are stronger than God."

"Does this mean that we're going back, Dad?" Liz asked.

Dr. Hunter was quiet for a long moment. Then he said, "A scripture comes to mind from Isaiah 30:21: 'Whether you turn to the right or to the left, your ears will hear a voice behind you, saying, "This is the way; walk in it."' We really need God's direction for our next steps."

In the darkness of the hut, Dr. Hunter held out his hands. His family and Paul gathered in a circle to pray.

Randal was getting used to this unusual tradition, though he couldn't see it made a difference. He had never heard God actually speak during prayer. But, taking Mrs. Hunter's hand on one side and Paul Wilks's on the other, he joined the circle.

Everyone stood quietly for several moments. Mrs. Hunter prayed, "Father, what is Your direction

31

for us? Should we go to the village without the medical supplies, or should we return to Manaus?"

There was silence again for another few moments. Then Paul Wilks prayed, followed by Dr. Hunter.

Suddenly Liz blurted out, "Hey, I just remembered the verse I read in my devotions this morning. And we talked about it in Sunday School last week."

Taking the flashlight from her father, she opened her backpack and found her Bible. After a few seconds of flipping, she found the verse. "Here it is. Philippians 4:13: 'I can do everything through him who gives me strength.' The apostle Paul was in jail when he wrote this. The verse helps me remember that even when things are tough, we can get through them. God is always with us."

"You're a good doctor, honey," said Mrs. Hunter. "Even without medical supplies I think God has a plan for us. And He has a plan for Avee, whatever that may be."

"Thanks," Dr. Hunter said, giving his daughter a hug. "That was the same verse the Lord had me focus on during my prayer time this morning."

"I think the Lord is directing us to go to the village," Mrs. Hunter said. "What do you think, Paul?"

"I agree. I know Kren meant this for evil, but I believe God intends to use it for good."

"So that's it, then. We're off to the village in the morning," Dr. Hunter said. "We better stretch out these hammocks and try to get some sleep."

Randal stood, looking puzzled. "You mean you believe God is directing us to go to the village because two people happened to read the same Bible verses this morning?"

Paul Wilks put his hand on the boy's shoulder and chuckled. "There are no coincidences in God's kingdom, my friend. You will see."

Along the path from the camp to the village, evil worked against the missionaries. Two figures hid a freshly dug pit. They laid sticks and leaves over its top. Hissing echoed from within.

7

Raven Ortega

Birds sang in the early morning air. Kren left the village with two men from his tribe as the sun peeped over the trees. They walked to a giant rubber tree with a jagged red star on its trunk.

The tree marked the beginning of what the Atroari called "the spirit land." Kren signaled for his companions to wait while he went on ahead. He didn't need to signal. Neither man dared to enter the jungle on the other side of the tree. They believed only a shaman could go there and live to tell about it. The evil spirits would destroy anyone else.

Kren moved quickly through the brush until he came to a stream. He swung over the stream, using one of the many low-hanging vines. A rocky mound sat before him. He climbed it with the ease of a leopard.

At the top, in a small clearing, stood four large tents. A man sat at a table in front of them, several maps spread before him. His large hands worked diligently, locating various spots of interest. Long, black hair fell over his shoulders and onto the table. Raven Ortega raised his head when he heard Kren approach.

He stared coolly at the shaman. People had called the man Raven since he was a teenager. The name was not given because of his hair. It was his eyes that everyone noticed. They were black and ruthless, like a raven's.

"Ah, Kren. You have good news, I hope," Raven Ortega said, speaking Kren's language perfectly.

"Kren always have good news," he said with a sly grin.

Ortega said nothing. His black eyes stared at Kren until he continued.

"Kren took away healing bag from the healer. Also set trap in jungle. Jungle spirits will chase white healer and family away. Kren will again be the most important person in the village."

Raven Ortega thought about Kren's report. He stood and paced back and forth with his hands behind his back. Then he stopped and faced Kren. "We have several more months of work before we finish the gold mining. We cannot have the authorities snooping around before we finish."

Kren nodded his head in agreement.

"We have been very good to you, Kren," Ortega continued. "We have given you many gifts that have made you powerful in the eyes of your people. We've even given you the powder that makes fire explode. In return you promised to keep people away from here. These missionaries could be very bad for our business. Do you understand?"

Kren started to speak, but Ortega continued.

"If your village listens to these missionaries about their God, then other missionaries will come. No one will listen to you anymore. You must stop them!" He slammed his fist on the table.

Ortega walked to a metal container, pulled out a small pouch, and tossed it to Kren.

"Here is more fire powder. Now go and do your job."

Kren opened the pouch and stuck his fingers inside. He felt the coarse, black powder. Smiling, he closed it and tied it to a leather strap around his waist.

"Kren will make missionaries go away." With that, he turned and left.

* * *

While Kren was speaking with Raven Ortega, the missionaries left the mission station for the Atroari village. Paul Wilks led the way, with Mrs. Hunter, Liz, Randal, and Josh following behind. Dr. Hunter brought up the rear. Although there was a path, the jungle brush grew so quickly that Paul often had to use his machete to clear the way.

"Look, a parrot," Liz said excitedly, pointing to the high limb of a tree just ahead. "Oh, it's beautiful."

"Elizabeth, that is a macaw, a blue macaw to be exact," Randal said, looking through a pair of binoculars. "It's one of many such species found in the tropical rain forest of Brazil."

"Look out," Liz said.

Josh did not see Randal stopped in front of him. He was too busy looking at the bird. They collided and fell.

"Joshua, would you mind watching where you are going? I am making some important observations of the birdlife in the area."

"Sorry, Randal. I didn't see you stop."

"Is everybody OK back there?" Paul stopped to ask.

Dr. Hunter helped the boys up. "Everything's fine back here, Paul; let's keep going."

When Paul and Mrs. Hunter stopped to look back at the boys, Liz kept walking. She went several meters ahead of the group. "Liz, you need to stay behind me on the trail," Paul said.

"I will. I just want to see what these flowers are," she said, walking toward a bushy tree with large, red blossoms.

Liz stepped toward it, but her foot caught a vine. Her body sprawled out, and she hit the ground. The dry leaves on the trail floor cushioned her fall. Humiliated, she scrambled to get back on her feet. When she pressed forward to push herself up, her hands disappeared into the ground. Hisses erupted from the hole. Liz screamed and jerked her hands out.

Paul had seen Liz fall and was just a few steps behind. "What's wrong, Liz?"

All Liz could do was point. He heard the hissing and pulled her away from the hole.

The others crowded around, but Paul motioned for them to stand back. He cut off a strong branch and removed the rest of the cover. Walking carefully to the edge of the pit, he looked down.

"Bushmasters," he said, stepping away from the hole. "They're deadly."

Liz clung to her mother. "If I hadn't tripped on the vine, I would have walked right into the pit," she said.

Dr. Hunter looked at Paul. "It was a trap," Paul said, answering his friend's question before he asked it. "Kren knew I would be in the lead. This was meant for me. I had no idea he would go this far."

"Should we turn back?" Dr. Hunter asked.

"If Kren is really trying to stop us, the mission station isn't safe either. We need to get to the chief at the village. We're about 20 minutes away."

Dr. Hunter nodded his agreement. With Paul leading, the missionaries hurried to the village, praying every step of the way.

8

The Challenge

"Wait!" Mrs. Hunter whispered. "Are those voices I hear ahead?"

Paul, a few steps in front, walked straight for a thick wall made of vines. Smiling, he said over his shoulder, "Yes, I believe those are voices."

Reaching into the wall, he grabbed one of the vines and pulled it back. An opening appeared through which Paul pointed. "We have arrived."

On the other side stood the Atroari village. Paul stepped through first. The others followed. A dozen huts, similar to those at the mission station, sat around a small clearing in the jungle. The village meeting place stood in the center. It was a large structure with a roof but no walls. Smoke from several cooking fires floated into the air, giving the village a hazy appearance.

When the Indians saw Paul, they stopped what they were doing. Excited voices filled the air. Many fingers pointed to the large meeting hut in the center of the village.

"I'm sure the chief has laid Avee, his son, in the central hut," Paul said to the Hunters. "You wait here while I go speak to him."

Josh, Liz, and Randal stared openmouthedly at the surroundings.

Liz never met a stranger. She smiled and waved. "Hi! My name's Liz."

A girl who looked Liz's age smiled back. An older woman standing close by put her arm around the girl's shoulders. She frowned at the strangers.

"Dad, the villagers don't look all that happy to see us," Josh said. "I thought they would be glad to have someone come to help the chief's son."

"Remember what Uncle Paul told us about Kren and his talk of angry spirits? The villagers probably aren't sure we're coming to help," Dr. Hunter said. He looked past Josh. "Randal, what in the world are you doing?"

Randal stood on one foot, holding one hand behind his back and the other on top of his head. He made a humming noise as he hopped from one foot to the other.

"It is a jungle greeting dance, of course. I read about it in one of my parents' research books," Randal answered. "I am telling the natives that we come in peace."

"Are you sure you read about the jungles of Brazil?" Josh asked. "They don't look as if they understand what you're doing."

"Maybe you're actually telling them we've come to eat their children," Liz teased.

The villagers just stood and looked at Randal with curiosity, then at each other. Finally an older

41

woman let out a cackling laugh that soon spread to all who were watching.

"See, they now understand we are peaceful and friendly. That's why they are laughing," Randal said with satisfaction.

Paul Wilks walked back and motioned for the Hunters to follow him. "Raoni (ray-AH-nee), the chief, wants to meet you. I told him about the stolen supplies and the snake pit," Paul said as they were walking. "He agrees that it's Kren. He also said Kren's talk of angry jungle spirits has frightened everyone in the village."

"No need to worry about the people being afraid of us, Mr. Wilks," Randal said. "I've just finished greeting them. They know we come in peace."

Paul chuckled. "Actually, Randal, from what I could understand, the villagers were laughing because they thought you looked like a giant monkey."

Randal felt his face grow hot. He glared at Josh and Liz. When they met his glare, they doubled over with laughter.

The group stopped in front of the large meeting hut. A man stood up from the shadows inside and walked out. He was shorter than Mr. Wilks, almost as short as Liz. Black hair laid in a bowl shape around his head. His large, brown eyes examined the strangers.

Paul Wilks spoke a few words to the man, then turned to the Hunters. "This is Raoni, the chief of this village."

Dr. Hunter gave a slight bow and smiled.

Raoni spoke a few words to Paul, who then turned and spoke again to the Hunters. "The chief says he is sorry that he cannot greet you in a proper way. But he has not left his son's side in two days."

"Tell him we understand, and ask him if I may examine his son," Dr. Hunter said.

Josh leaned close to Liz and whispered, "Do you smell something burning?"

"Yes. It smells like—"

KABOOM!

An explosion of fire and black smoke erupted from a cooking fire just behind them. Screams erupted from the villagers.

Out of the black smoke, a man appeared. A pointy grin covered his face. The jagged scar above his lip twisted like a worm on a fishhook.

Paul looked at Dr. Hunter. "Kren," he said.

Kren began talking rapidly to the villagers, who gathered around him. He leaped into the air, gesturing wildly with his arms as he spoke.

Paul interpreted for the Hunters. "I don't understand everything he's saying. Something about the jungle spirits being angry at the arrival of strangers. He says the spirits will hurt more children in the village unless the people force us to leave."

When Kren had finished, several of the Atroari men grabbed their blowguns and pointed them toward the Hunters. But the chief held up his hand to calm the villagers.

Paul stepped out into the area where Kren stood. He spoke a simple sentence, first in English, then in the Atroari language. "We serve the one and only God, and He is stronger than any jungle spirit."

Kren laughed shrilly after hearing Paul's words. "Then let your God heal Avee," he said.

44

9

Is It True?

"He said what?!" Dr. Hunter whispered excitedly after Paul interpreted Kren's words. "Do you understand what that means? If we can't help Avee, they're going to start pointing their blowguns at us again."

"Dad," interrupted Liz.

"Not now, Liz."

"Paul, did you forget? I have no medical supplies. When you said our God was stronger than his spirits, you played right into Kren's hands."

"Dad," said Liz again.

"Liz, I told you, not now."

But seeing that his words were sharper than he intended, Dr. Hunter turned to his daughter. "I'm sorry, Lizzy; what did you want to say?"

"I just want to know if what Uncle Paul said to Kren was true."

Dr. Hunter stood quietly, looking at his daughter. Then he looked at Josh and Randal and his wife. He felt ashamed for the way he had been talking.

"Yes, Lizzy, Uncle Paul's words were 100 percent true. Thanks for reminding me."

"Remember God's Word," Liz said. "'I can do everything through him who gives me strength.'"

Dr. Hunter smiled. He thought about the apostle Paul and his hardship. He thought about how God takes care of us, no matter what. Then he looked up at his wife and Paul and said, "Let's have a look at Avee."

Paul spoke a few words to the chief, who turned, motioning for everyone to follow.

"Dear, should the children wait outside?" Mrs. Hunter asked.

"No. I think we all have a part in this now."

Mrs. Hunter nodded in agreement, then told the children to follow quietly.

Even without walls, the hut was dark. The small fire burning in the center cast more shadows than light. A young boy lay on a mat next to the fire. Two women sat next to him. One held his hand. The other fanned away insects with a large leaf.

The chief stood over Avee and spoke to the women. After a moment, they stood and moved away.

"That's Avee's mother and sister," Paul explained.

Dr. and Mrs. Hunter knelt on either side of Avee and carefully examined him. He moaned softly when their hands touched his injuries. They spoke quietly to one another as they worked.

After 10 minutes of examining, with several questions to Raoni that Paul interpreted, the Hunters stood.

"There is no swelling or discoloration around his head and neck. That's good," Dr. Hunter said. "His hip is either broken or badly dislocated, as is his left

shoulder. That's why he won't move. It is very painful. He's also suffering from shock."

"Can we take him back to Manaus?" Paul asked.

"I don't think his back is broken. But without X rays, I can't be sure. I have no medicine to give him for the pain. I'm afraid the shock of such a trip might be too much for him."

"Is there anything we can do?" asked Paul.

"We can put his shoulder back in place. We can try to align his hip too. If it's dislocated, that should fix it. But if it's broken, it will be very painful. We'll just have to see how he responds to know if his back is broken."

Paul talked with the chief. After talking and motioning to each other, Paul turned back to Dr. Hunter.

"Avee is too weak to take out of the village," Paul said. "The chief wants us to help him here if we can. Fix his shoulder, and try to fix his hip too. The chief knows it will be painful for Avee. But there is no other choice."

Dr. and Mrs. Hunter worked on Avee. They fixed his shoulder, but they could not fix his leg. He screamed every time they tried. Dr. Hunter turned to Paul. "I really think his hip is broken. I hope we didn't hurt him more than we helped."

Josh looked around. He noticed the whole village had surrounded the hut. They were waiting to see what would happen.

Randal knew what was coming next. It was time to pray. Yet he didn't mind this time. Like the villagers outside, he wanted to see what would happen.

Dr. Hunter knelt beside Avee. He motioned for everyone to join him. He and Paul gently laid their hands on Avee's head. Outside, the villagers looked on in silence. Curious faces watched the group kneel in the hut. The jungle grew strangely quiet.

The missionaries' prayers were simple. They asked their Heavenly Father to heal Avee in a way that would bring glory to Jesus. They prayed silently for a long time. Dr. Hunter was about to say Amen when Liz began to pray softly. "Father, Your Word says that You are our Strength. Please be Avee's Strength too. Please make him well so he can hear how much You love him."

"Father, we pray this in the name of Jesus. Amen," Dr. Hunter said.

Slowly the group stood. Avee was sleeping now. His breathing was even and steady. Paul walked over to the chief, who stood at the edge of the hut. The others joined him. Suddenly someone in the crowd of villagers started yelling. The crowd parted, and Kren came forward. He pointed his finger at the missionaries as he screamed.

Paul and Dr. Hunter came out of the hut to face him. "He's screaming that our God has no power," Paul said to his friend.

"Any suggestions on what we do now?" Dr. Hunter asked.

"I'm not sure, but . . ."

Paul stopped talking. Dr. Hunter noticed Paul was staring strangely at Kren. Kren was standing in silence, his mouth open. Both men turned around to see what had grabbed Kren's attention.

There, standing on his own power at the edge of the hut, was Avee.

10

Joy

The villagers stood silently as they stared at Avee. Then a burst of joyous shouts and clapping broke the silence. The celebration began.

Raoni picked up his son, holding him tightly. He walked into the crowd of cheering Indians. Tears of joy and thanksgiving ran down the faces of all the Hunters.

Paul kept shouting, "Thank You, Jesus! Thank You, Jesus!" Even Randal felt emotion swelling in his chest.

Suddenly the noise from the villagers stopped. The whole tribe turned to face the missionaries. One by one they got down on their knees and bowed in worship. Paul rushed forward. He gently raised one of the men in front to his feet. Then Paul motioned for everyone else to do the same.

"My friends, please stand up. We are all men and women just like you. Do not worship us. We were not the ones that showed mercy to Avee today. It was Jesus."

Paul kept speaking to the people. He had trouble with the language. But he still shared a simple gospel message. The eyes of the crowd focused on him. When he finished, Mrs. Hunter took her husband's hand and smiled. It was obvious to her that the Spirit of God had touched the villagers.

"Does this mean that everyone in the village will follow Jesus?" Josh asked.

"We don't know, Son," Dr. Hunter answered. "But they've all heard the Good News. The Lord doesn't always heal people as miraculously as He healed Avee. These people have seen the power of God. Now they must decide to believe it."

It was a long time before Raoni and Avee could break away from the villagers and speak with the Hunters. As Avee walked toward them, Dr. Hunter marveled at what he saw. His examination had been correct. The only way Avee could be walking right now was by the touch of God.

Paul interpreted words of thanks from the chief and his son to the Hunters. Then he asked, "Where is Kren? In all the excitement, I lost track of him."

"I saw him run from the village with a few men," Josh said.

The chief began to discuss something with Paul. After a few moments, Paul turned to talk with the Hunters.

"One of the villagers has seen strangers in the area. He said they were doing some kind of digging. He saw Kren with them."

"Who else could be in the area?" Mrs. Hunter asked.

"My best guess would be illegal gold miners. Gold was discovered in Brazil in the late 1980s. Thou-

sands of people flooded the area, trying to get rich. A few did. The Brazilian government finally ran everyone out."

"Why would Kren get involved with gold miners?" Dr. Hunter asked.

"They may be using him to keep the villagers away from their mine. In turn they give him gifts that make him look powerful in front of his people. That would explain why he did not want me here."

"If that's true, Paul, we may be dealing with something a lot bigger than an angry shaman," Dr. Hunter said. "People protecting their gold can be very dangerous. We need to get the authorities involved right away."

"I agree. We need to get back to the radio at the mission station as soon as possible," said Paul. "It's 2 P.M. If we leave now, we can reach camp before dark."

* * *

Raven Ortega's black eyes narrowed with hatred. He listened as Kren told the story of Avee's healing. Christian missionaries—he hated them. They had caused trouble like this before. He was too close to the gold to stop this time.

"You are a fool, Kren," Ortega hissed, barely able to contain his rage. "Now I must step in and finish your job." He spat on the ground. "I should have handled them myself from the beginning."

Ortega spoke to one of his men. "Shan, they'll be heading back to the mission station next. Take four of your men and follow Kren there." He thought for a moment. "Destroy their radio first. Then show them what happens when the jungle spirits really get angry." A growling laugh escaped his twisted mouth.

11

Protection

Paul did not lead the way on the return trip to the mission station. Raoni sent six men to accompany the missionaries. The chief knew there would be trouble.

"Do you think Kren will come after us, Dad?" Josh asked over his shoulder.

"If he does, it will be at the mission station tonight. Those who do evil like to hide in the darkness. I don't believe he'll try anything during daylight."

Josh walked in silence for a while, then spoke to Randal, who was just in front of him. "Hey, Randal, you sure have been quiet."

"Actually, Joshua, I find myself at a loss for words," Randal replied.

Josh said nothing, waiting for his cousin to continue.

"I've gone to church all my life. I've memorized lots of Bible verses in Sunday School. And I've known more Bible stories than the teachers. Until this trip, I thought that's all they were—just stories. To me the

Bible was an interesting book; God took no part in day-to-day life." Randal started to say more but noticed everyone ahead had come to a halt.

The three men leading the way stopped, talking rapidly to the three at the end of the line. One turned to speak to Paul, then began moving at a much quicker pace.

"What was that all about?" Mrs. Hunter asked.

"They say someone is following us," Paul answered. "They don't think they're trying to catch us, just keeping us in sight. We need to get to the mission station as fast as we can. If we walk faster, we can be there in 15 or 20 minutes."

* * *

Fifty meters behind the missionaries, Kren hid in the jungle. Two of his three men, with the four gold miners sent by Raven Ortega, lay hidden beside him.

"They know we are here," Kren said to the men. He chuckled to himself. "It is good that they know we are following. It makes the hunt much more fun."

Shan, Ortega's man, moved up next to Kren. "One of your men has already gone to destroy their radio. Let's attack before they get to their camp," he said.

Kren stood, motioning the others to follow. "The spirits have shown Kren the time. We will wait for the dark. Then all will know who has the power."

* * *

As Paul had said, they arrived at the mission station within 20 minutes. The men from the village immediately spread out around the camp area to watch for signs of trouble. They had their spears and blowguns ready.

Paul looked at Josh. "You, Liz, and Randal break up some of the wood in that pile over there. Help your dad and mom get a fire going," he said. "You'll find an ax in the tent. I'm going to try to radio the authorities."

Dr. and Mrs. Hunter cleared burnt wood from the fire pit. Josh used the ax to chop some dried limbs in the brush pile. Liz was the first to notice Paul return. He talked quietly to her parents. His face was drawn into a frown.

"That was a quick radio message, Uncle Paul," she said.

After a long silence, Dr. Hunter said, "It looks like we won't be using the radio for a while."

Josh and Randal stopped working. "Why? What's wrong with the radio?" Josh asked.

"One of Kren's men got here first. It looks like someone took a rock and beat it to pieces," Paul answered.

The first shadows of nightfall crept across the camp.

"What are we going to do now?" Liz asked.

"The supply boat should be here tomorrow or the next day," Paul said. "It will have a radio on board. For now let's get this fire going. I'll alert the other men to keep a close watch."

"OK, let's get to it," Dr. Hunter said, clapping his hands. He knew that they all needed to stay busy, or fear would take over their thinking.

"Excuse me, but aren't we forgetting something?" Randal said.

Mrs. Hunter's eyes brightened as she looked over at her nephew, who was a little embarrassed.

"I think Randal means, shouldn't we pray before we do anything else?" she said.

If it had been another place or time, Josh and Liz might have fainted. But under the circumstances, the group just smiled as they grabbed each other's hands and prayed for God's protection.

* * *

Darkness settled over the jungle. Screeches and chatter filled the night air. From atop a hill, Kren and his men looked down at the mission station. The time had come to get rid of the intruders. Kren hoped the village men would turn and run as soon as he attacked. He had no desire to fight his own people.

Kren and his men began their descent, but suddenly one of the men grabbed his arm. The man pointed a shaky finger toward the camp. Kren gazed in the same direction, at first seeing nothing. Then he saw them; he felt the hair on his neck rise like a porcupine's. Soldiers!

"Where did they come from?" he hissed.

Two soldiers stood on either side of the fire. Several others were stationed around the camp, facing the jungle. Without warning one of the soldiers pointed directly to where Kren and his men were hiding. He gave a loud shout and began a charge to where they were hiding, followed by the other soldiers.

Kren and his men shielded their eyes from the increasing light. Then they turned in terror and fled.

12

A Hole in the Darkness

An early morning mist floated off the river, hovering just above the ground. Paul Wilks and Dr. Hunter sat by the fire, each with a cup of lukewarm coffee in his hands. Mrs. Hunter sat next to her husband, her arm around Liz, who was waking up.

"Is it morning yet?" Liz said groggily.

Josh and Randal had tried to stay awake and keep watch, but both had fallen asleep. Liz's question caused them to stir also.

"Yes, it's morning," Paul replied. He chuckled at the confused look on the boys' faces as they tried to remember where they were.

Josh sat up suddenly. "Hey, we're OK! Kren never attacked."

"Evidently," Dr. Hunter said. "The men from the village said they heard some rustling in the jungle late last night. But they didn't see anything."

Just then, several of the men came running toward the fire, followed by another group from the village.

"It's Raoni and Avee," Paul said. He stood to greet them.

Raoni walked up to Paul. He touched his shoulder—the village custom for greetings. Avee stood behind, grinning broadly.

At first Paul had difficulty understanding what Raoni was trying to say. Finally, he turned to the others with a curious look on his face.

"Raoni wants to know where our warriors are."

"Warriors? Does he mean the men from the village?" Dr. Hunter asked.

"No. He says three of the men following Kren came running back to the village late last night, terrified. They told the chief that they had hidden just outside our camp, ready to attack. Suddenly soldiers were standing all around us. They chased the men all the way back to the village."

"You're sure he said soldiers?" Mrs. Hunter asked.

Before answering, Paul talked to Raoni again.

"Yes, he said soldiers. Big soldiers."

"Dad, did soldiers come last night while I was asleep?" Liz asked.

There was a long silence before Dr. Hunter answered. "Not soldiers we could see, Liz. The Lord answered our prayer for protection. He sent His soldiers to watch over us."

"You mean angels?" Randal asked.

"That's what it sounds like," Dr. Hunter said, shaking his head in amazement.

"Wow! Angels!" Liz said. "Why didn't someone wake me? I missed them."

"We all did, sweetheart," Mrs. Hunter said. "Even if you'd been awake, you wouldn't have seen them."

Raoni had a curious look on his face. Paul began to explain to him about the warriors. When Raoni finally spoke, he did so very slowly with tears in his eyes. Rather than waiting for Raoni to finish, Paul began translating as he spoke.

"Raoni says that we have much to learn about the customs of his people. But he says we have proven to be friends and have shown that we know the true God."

Raoni dropped to his knees. Avee followed him. Paul continued to speak.

"Raoni says they are not bowing to us but to our God. They want to know if what I have told them is true. They want to know God too."

Paul smiled as he knelt beside his friends. The other Atroari tribesmen stood quietly and watched. Paul led father and son in a simple prayer that introduced them to the King of the universe.

When they had finished, Randal looked at Dr. Hunter. "Uncle Lee, I think it's about time I knew God too."

The faint sound of the supply boat chugging up the river came as Randal knelt to pray, surrounded by his family.

Epilogue

Randal finished stuffing the last of his clothes into his suitcase. Two weeks earlier he and the Hunters had returned to Oklahoma from the Work and Witness trip. He was leaving to go home early the next morning.

"Hey, you three! Last call to wash up and get down here for dinner," Mrs. Hunter called from the kitchen downstairs.

As everyone sat down, Liz noticed a letter sitting on her dad's plate. She saw that the postmark was from Brazil.

"Dad, is that a letter from Uncle Paul?" she asked excitedly.

Dr. Hunter smiled mischievously. "I don't know, Lizzy. Let's eat and find out later."

He knew it would drive his daughter crazy.

"No, Dad, you've got to read it! I can't eat if you don't!"

"OK, let's read it before we eat."

Everyone at the table cheered. Dr. Hunter couldn't wait to read it either.

Dear Lee, Rusti, Josh, Liz, and Randal,

You left too quickly on the supply boat that last day. I didn't get a chance to tell you how much your being with us blessed our lives here in the village.

The Brazilian authorities came the day after

you left. Sure enough, there were illegal gold miners. We found their camp, but no miners. Hopefully they left the country.

We haven't seen Kren since the night he ran from the mission station. My guess is he's still running. However, I'm praying for him. I figure he qualifies as one of the enemies we're supposed to pray for.

Some of the Bible translators are helping me in the village. We hope to have a chapter from the Gospel of John translated by the end of the year. It's slow work, but Raoni and Avee have been a great help.

We now have an official church in the village. Fifteen people have given their hearts to Jesus. Isn't God GREAT!

Well, I need to go. I'll write when I can. Start planning your next trip down here.

Love,

Paul

"Dad, do you think Kren really is still running through the jungle?" Liz asked.

"I don't know, Lizzy. But I agree with Paul—we need to pray for him."

"Speaking of praying," Mrs. Hunter said, "we need to bless this food before it gets cold."

Dr. Hunter smiled and looked at his nephew. "Randal, would you do the honors tonight?"